FOOTBALL
How It Works

The Science of Sports The Science of Sports

Sports
Illustrated
KID$

BY AGNIESZKA BISKUP

CAPSTONE PRESS
a capstone imprint

Sports Illustrated KIDS The Science of Sports is published by Capstone Press,
151 Good Counsel Drive, P.O. Box 669, Mankato, Minnesota 56002.
www.capstonepress.com

012010
005669R

Books published by Capstone Press are manufactured with paper
containing at least 10 percent post-consumer waste.

Library of Congress Cataloging-in-Publication Data
Biskup, Agnieszka.
    Football : how it works / by Agnieszka Biskup.
    p. cm. — (Sports Illustrated KIDS. The Science of Sports)
    Includes bibliographical references and index.
    Summary: "Describes the science behind the sport of football, including offense, defense, special
teams, and arenas" — Provided by publisher.
    ISBN 978-1-4296-4022-0 (library binding)
    ISBN 978-1-4296-4875-2 (paperback)
    1. Football — Juvenile literature. I. Title. II. Series.
GV950.7.B57 2010
796.332 — dc22   2009032782

Editorial Credits
Mandy Robbins, editor; Ted Williams, designer; Jo Miller, media researcher;
    Eric Manske, production specialist

* Capstone Press would like to thank Brian Kokos, science teacher and football coach for
Blue Earth Area Schools for his help in creating this book.

Design Elements
Shutterstock/Eray Haciosmanoglu; kamphi

Photo Credits
Getty Images Inc./Al Pereira, 1; Andy Lyons, 12; Bryan Mitchell, 16; Dilip Vishwanat, 40–41;
    Donald Miralle, 13 (both); Joe Robbins, 24–25; Otto Greul, 29; Paul Spinelli, 27, 34;
    Rex Brown, 26; Tom Hauck, 17
Shutterstock/Danny E Hooks, cover (diagram); Filip Fuxa, cover (background);
    Richard Sargeant, cover (football field); Todd Taulman, cover (clipped football)
Sports Illustrated/Al Tielemans, 18, 31 (bottom), 32 (bottom); Bill Frakes, 9, 14–15; Bob Rosato,
    cover (bottom right), 15, 38, 39, 44; Damian Strohmeyer, 22, 23; David E. Klutho, 35;
    John Biever, cover (bottom center), 3, 8, 10–11, 42, 43; John W. McDonough, cover (main photo);
    Peter Read Miller, 6, 33; Robert Beck, 31 (top), 36; Simon Bruty, cover (bottom left), 4–5,
    7 (footballs), 19, 20, 21, 30, 32 (top), 37

TABLE OF CONTENTS

What's behind every bone-crushing tackle, every soaring kick, and every breathtaking pass? Science! Football is a game of mass, motion, and collisions. The big hits are part of what makes the game so exciting. The forces involved can get pretty wild. For example, picture two players colliding helmet-to-helmet. That impact can have the same force as being hit with a 16-pound (7.3-kilogram) bowling ball from 12 feet (3.7 meters).

center of gravity
A player positions his body around his center of gravity to stay balanced when crouching low.

Of course, those amazing long passes aren't too shabby either! Quarterbacks may not be thinking about it as they do it, but they're using science every time they throw the ball. Science helps explain why players move the way they do and why the ball acts the way it does.

momentum
The player gains momentum when he begins to move down the field.

friction
The players use friction between their cleats and the ground to push off against the field.

The offensive goal in football seems simple: score. But scientific factors affect how players move the ball up the field.

The circumference of a ball is the distance measured around its widest points.

BALL BASICS

A football's unique shape has some important effects on the game. It is shaped to be **AERODYNAMIC**. When thrown correctly, the pointy end of the ball meets less resistance as it slices through the air.

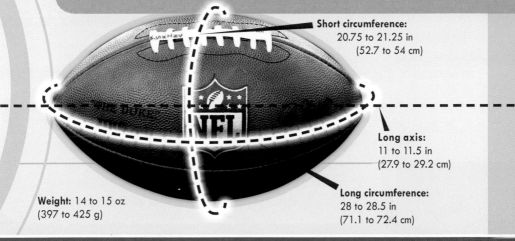

The National Football League (NFL) has strict rules about the size of the football. A regulation football has specific dimensions.

Short circumference:
20.75 to 21.25 in
(52.7 to 54 cm)

Long axis:
11 to 11.5 in
(27.9 to 29.2 cm)

Long circumference:
28 to 28.5 in
(71.1 to 72.4 cm)

Weight: 14 to 15 oz
(397 to 425 g)

ASKING ABOUT AXES

An axis is an imaginary line between two points. It runs through the center of an object. A football has two axes. One is short and runs parallel to the **EQUATOR** in the fat center of the ball. The other is long and goes from pole to pole through the pointy ends of the ball.

A baseball is a sphere. In a sphere, the axes are all the same length. A football's shape is called a prolate spheroid. In a prolate spheroid, the axis that goes from pole to pole is longer than the axis that goes through the equator. A discus, on the other hand, is an oblate spheroid. The axis that goes through the equator is longer than the axis that goes from pole to pole.

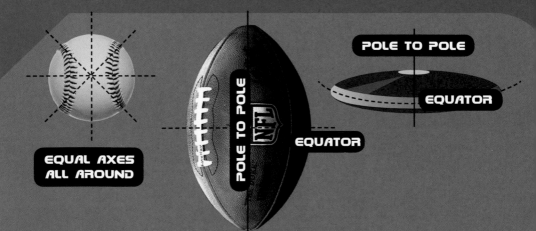

POLE TO POLE

EQUATOR

POLE TO POLE

EQUATOR

EQUAL AXES
ALL AROUND

AERODYNAMIC — designed to move easily through the air
EQUATOR — an imaginary line around the middle of a rounded object

7

Good quarterbacks throw the football in a way that makes it easier for receivers to catch it. A football must be thrown with force and speed. The quarterback wants to make sure that the ball doesn't drop too early. He also wants to make sure that a defensive player doesn't have time to **INTERCEPT** the ball.

To control the throw, the quarterback's hand needs to be close to the ball's **CENTER OF GRAVITY**, which is near the ball's middle. But he also needs to hold the ball as far back as he can to throw it with more force. A quarterback's grip on the ball is a compromise between these two factors.

center of gravity

A quarterback needs arm strength. The stronger he is, the faster and farther he'll be able to throw the ball.

PROJECTILE MOTION

The force of gravity influences the movement of a football in the air. A football travels in a curve called a parabolic arc. As the ball travels up, gravity slows it down until it reaches its peak height. Then gravity pulls it down, and the ball starts accelerating toward the ground.

INTERCEPT — when a defensive player catches an offensive pass
CENTER OF GRAVITY — the point on an object at which it can balance

SPIN DOCTORS

A well-thrown football travels in a spiral motion. To pass effectively, a quarterback must throw the ball so that it spins around its long axis. This creates a **GYROSCOPIC** effect. The same effect is in a spinning top. A gyroscope that spins really fast is very stable. It can resist forces like wind. The faster the football spins, the more stable its path is. A stable path makes the throw more accurate.

Not all passes are thrown just right. Throwing a perfect pass requires a lot of coordination and timing. The quarterback is usually throwing to where he thinks a receiver will be by the time the ball gets there. And if the ball's spin is off, it will start wobbling and go off target.

solid spinning throw
A ball thrown with a strong spin will travel in a stable path.

tumbling ball
A ball thrown with a weak spin will tumble.

GYROSCOPIC — describes an object that spins inside a frame and causes the frame to balance in any position

CATCHING THE BALL

Catching a football is actually pretty remarkable. A receiver has to figure out where to be just by watching the football in flight. A receiver's focus and body position all have to be in sync. He needs to follow the ball with his eyes from the moment it leaves the quarterback's hands until he catches it. At the same time, he has to figure out his ideal body and arm position for the catch. He also has to dodge players ready to bring him down.

Eli Manning

A football's shape makes it easier for a player to carry than a round ball. It can be tucked between the arm and rib cage, making a fumble less likely.

David Tyree

In Super Bowl XLII, David Tyree caught Eli Manning's pass against his helmet!

66It was just a great catch by David Tyree. I found a way to get loose, and just really threw it up. He made an unbelievable catch and saved the game.99 — Eli Manning

RUNNING THE BALL

Speed and quickness are not the same thing. Quickness is **ACCELERATION** and the ability to change direction fast. Players need quickness to dodge opponents and speed to outrun them.

momentum = mass x velocity

Speed is necessary for open-field running. When a player runs in an open field, he can reach his maximum momentum. Momentum is the product of **MASS** times **VELOCITY**. It gives a player the power to charge through his opponents. A heavier player moving at a slower speed can have the same momentum as a lighter player moving more quickly.

ACCELERATION — the rate of change of velocity
MASS — the amount of material in an object
VELOCITY — a measurement of both the speed and direction an object is moving

Great receivers and running backs have an ability to "see the holes" as they run down the field. They find the path of least resistance to make the play and gain important yardage.

JUKING IT OUT

Another talent that good receivers and running backs share is juking. Juking is a quick change in direction to fake out an opponent. Juking helps players avoid being tackled. Unfortunately, it can also lead to ankle and knee problems. Moving quickly from side to side puts a huge amount of force on a player's legs. The force can be especially hard on delicate ankle joints.

RUNNING BACKS: JACKS OF ALL TRADES

A running back's job is to get the ball down the field any way possible. Running backs catch, block, run, and sometimes even pass the ball. Science helps guide how different people play this position. Shorter, lighter players, like Barry Sanders, are generally quicker. They also tend to have a lower center of gravity. These players juke their way around their opponents and scramble up the field. They are nicknamed "scat backs." Scat backs typically run side to side as they move up the field.

Barry Sanders

T.J. Duckett

T.J. Duckett and Jerome Bettis were larger running backs who used their mass to gain momentum. These types of players plow over their opponents. They are often called "power backs." Power backs usually run straight up the field.

Adrian Peterson is a running back with both quickness and mass. He can juke with the best of them. But his size helps him run straight through his opponents too.

Some teams have both types of running backs. They'll put their scat back in until the team gets close to the goal line. Then the power back will come in and charge through the defense to score.

	Height	Weight
Barry Sanders	5 ft, 8 in (1 m, 73 cm)	203 pounds (92 kilograms)
T.J. Duckett	6 ft (1 m, 83 cm)	254 pounds (115 kilograms)
Jerome Bettis	5 ft, 11 in (1 m, 80 cm)	255 pounds (116 kilograms)
Adrian Peterson	6 ft, 1 in (1 m, 85 cm)	217 pounds (98 kilograms)

The goal of defense is simple: stop the other team from scoring. At the beginning of every play, linemen face off against each other. Defensive linemen want to stop the other team's forward movement.

THE LINE OF DEFENSE

Why do coaches want linemen to be so heavy and wide? Linemen need to be difficult to move. The more mass something has, the more inertia it has. Newton's first law of motion explains inertia.

NEWTON'S FIRST LAW OF MOTION

A body at rest will stay at rest, unless acted on by some outside force. A body in motion will stay in motion, unless acted on by some outside force.

Linemen crouch low so that their **CENTER OF MASS** is closer to the ground. This makes it harder for an opposing player to knock them out of the way.

To take down opponents, linemen need to build momentum. Since momentum = mass x velocity, linemen have to increase mass or velocity to increase momentum. Linemen don't have much room to increase their velocity, so it's important for them to be massive.

CENTER OF MASS — the point in a body at which most of the mass is concentrated; below that point, a body is easier to topple.

19

TACKLING

Coaches tell players to hit low and keep their legs pumping. They want players to hit below an opponent's center of mass. Hitting low makes the opponent easier to knock down. When tackling, players keep pumping their legs on the ground to create more force and to stay balanced.

Momentum is important for blocking and tackling. A lighter player moving with greater velocity can push back a slower but heavier player. But if the two players collide at the same velocity, the lighter player will be driven back.

The average lineman today is about 100 pounds (45 kilograms) heavier than the average lineman in 1920. More mass gives them more momentum and makes them even harder to move or stop.

HARD HITS

Players experience enormous forces in a hit. But because it only lasts a split-second, the body can withstand it. The most dangerous hits occur in the open field. Linebackers and defensive backs create huge momentum when they increase their velocity to tackle running backs and receivers. Linemen, on the other hand, stand shoulder-to-shoulder with each other and face-to-face with their opponents. They don't have as much room to speed up before a hit. Because of this, their collisions aren't as violent, and their injury rates are usually lower.

G-FORCE

G-force is the force of gravity on the acceleration of a body. In a weightless environment, such as free fall, the g-force of an object is zero. On Earth, a stationary object has a g-force of 1. You can experience more g-force by accelerating. Some roller coasters can put 5 gs of force on your body. Football players can experience an amazing 150 gs during a hard hit.

g-force per event

0 10 20 30 40 50 60 70 80 90 100 110 120 130 140 150

Walking: 1

Sneezing: 2

Shuttle launch: 3

Coughing: 3.5

Roller coaster: 5

F-16 fighter jet roll: 9

Concussion: 100

Extreme football impact: 150

CHAPTER 3

SPECIAL TEAMS

The most visible players during a football game play offense and defense. But special teams also play an important role. They are the athletes who handle the kicking portion of the game. A football game can be won or lost by one kick.

PUNTING

A punter needs good coordination. He drops the ball and kicks it as it falls. The timing of the drop with his swinging foot is very important. If his timing is off, the kick might not be effective. Its **HANG TIME** or **RANGE** might be affected.

The punter wants to kick the ball as far as possible, while keeping it in the air as long as possible. The longer the ball is in the air, the more time his teammates have to get to and tackle the punt returner.

But getting the best hang time and the longest distance cancel each other out. To get the maximum of either, one needs to be sacrificed. To get maximum range, you have to launch the football at an angle of 45 degrees. To get maximum hang time, a punter would kick the ball at a 90-degree angle. But that would kick the ball straight up, and the ball wouldn't get very far. So punters have to compromise. There may be a wide variety of angles a punter ends up using, all depending on the wind and weather conditions.

90 degrees

45 degrees

HANG TIME — how long the ball hangs in the air once it is kicked

RANGE — the distance a football is kicked

KICKING FIELD GOALS

Placekicking is different from punting because the ball is teed or held rather than dropped. The kicker usually takes a running start to build up speed. He plants his non-kicking foot. Then he brings his kicking leg forward with a slight bend at the knee. Just as his foot makes contact with the ball, his kicking leg snaps straight. This quick motion transfers energy from the foot to the ball. The foot is in contact with the ball for about eight one-thousandths of a second. In that short time, up to 1 ton of force is applied to the ball.

Two kickers share the NFL record for the longest successful field goal, which is 63 yards (58 meters). Straight-style kicker Tom Dempsey of the New Orleans Saints kicked one in 1970. Jason Elam of the Denver Broncos, a soccer-style kicker, kicked the other in 1998.

KICKING WITH STYLE

There are two types of kicks: straight style and soccer style. Straight-style kickers kick the ball straight on. Soccer-style kickers come at the ball from a 45-degree angle.

Traditionally, kickers used the straight style. But with the growing popularity of soccer, more kickers changed to soccer style. Today, coaches and players believe that soccer-style kicking provides more power and accuracy. All NFL kickers use a soccer-style approach.

The soccer-style kick is more accurate because more of the foot's surface makes contact with the ball. This extra contact gives the kicker more control over where the ball goes.

KICKING PROBLEMS

Extreme temperatures can affect kicking distances. A kicked football will travel slightly farther in hot air than it will in very cold air. Cold temperatures make air molecules stick closer together. This makes the air **DENSER**. Denser air puts more air resistance on the ball.

Rain and wind affect kicking too. Rainy weather can force the kicker to shorten his stride to keep from slipping as he approaches the ball. A shorter stride makes for a shorter kick. Wind can hurt or help a kick depending on which direction it's blowing from.

TRUTH OR MYTH: ICING THE KICKER

Coaches sometimes call a time-out when the game is on the line and the opponents are setting up a field goal attempt. This is called "icing the kicker." They hope that by making the kicker wait, they'll mess up his concentration and cause his field goal attempt to fail.

But does it really work? Statisticians Scott Berry and Craig Wood studied data about field goal attempts during the 2002 and 2003 season. From their research, it appears that a kicker does have a slightly smaller chance of making the goal if he has to wait to make a kick.

DENSITY — how heavy or light an object is for its size; density is measured by dividing an object's mass by its volume.

CHAPTER 4

▷ GEAR UP

Almost every part of a player's body is covered by some kind of protective equipment or gear. The gear works like a suit of armor to help shield a player's body from bone-jarring hits.

Football players wear a lot of protective padding: shoulder pads, hip pads, thigh pads, and knee pads. Padding helps absorb energy from a hit. It also slows the speed of impact. A slower hit will generate less force.

Players also have fun with protective gear. They enjoy slamming into each other to celebrate a successful play.

Quarterbacks wear flak jackets under their jerseys. Flak jackets are made of light foam padding and are covered in plastic. They spread out the force of a hit to help prevent broken ribs.

Shoulder pads have a hard plastic outer covering. This covering helps spread the impact of a blow over a larger area. Shoulder pad plastic hasn't changed much over the years. But today's pads are molded into designs with more right angles. These angles help deflect impacts better.

Modern padding is made of visco elastic foam, also known as memory foam. Memory foam rebounds more rapidly after hits than regular foam does.

Hip and knee pads help protect the pelvis and knees in hard falls.

HANDS AND FEET

Players wear different types of gloves to help them play better. Receivers wear gloves with sticky palms to provide more friction. This friction helps them grip the ball better.

Some quarterbacks also wear gloves to help grip the ball better. Others prefer not to wear gloves. These players think they get a better grip on the ball with bare hands.

Linemen's gloves are heavily padded on the top of the hand and wrist. The padding absorbs some of the force as linemen fight off opposing players.

SHOES

Wearing the right shoes for the right conditions helps prevent injuries. Football games are played on regular grass and on artificial surfaces. The surface can be icy, wet, dry, or damp. Different types of shoes help players perform their best for each type of surface. Players even change shoes as weather conditions change.

In wet conditions, players wear shoes with heavier soles. This gives them more traction on slippery ground.

Players wear cleats on grass. These shoes have sharp knobs on their soles. The metal or plastic knobs dig into the ground, providing more grip. Shorter cleats are used for dry conditions. Cleats up to 1 inch (2.5 centimeters) long are used for very wet or icy conditions.

Cleats can cause problems too. They can cause injuries when a player quickly changes direction or makes a sudden stop. In these instances, the player's feet stick to the ground, while his body continues moving. The force puts extra strain on knee and ankle joints.

HEAD GEAR

Perhaps the most important piece of a football player's equipment is his helmet. It helps prevent serious head injuries by absorbing energy from a hit. A helmet is made up of a hard shell, face mask, chin strap, mouth guard, and cushioning jaw pads and air bladders.

Helmets are carefully fitted to hug each player's head exactly. A helmet that is too tight or too loose can make injuries more likely.

Foam and inflatable air pads inside the helmet customize the fit and provide cushioning. The padding keeps the player's head from accelerating too quickly upon being hit. The hard shell works to help distribute the force of a hit over a wider area.

A face mask shields a player's eyes and face from hard hits. Face masks come in a variety of styles to suit various players. Some players, like quarterbacks and receivers, have face masks that provide good visibility. Other players, like linemen, choose masks that offer more protection. Mouth guards help protect the teeth by spreading an impact to the mouth over a larger area.

Coaches communicate directly with their quarterbacks through radios in the quarterbacks' helmets.

CHAPTER 5

▷ STAYING FIT AND SAFE

Football is an extremely demanding sport.
Exercise and weight training make players strong
and less likely to get injured.

TOUGH TRAINING

Professional football players don't just train during the football
season. Players stay in shape all year long. They weight train to
strengthen their muscles. Well-developed muscles help protect
bones from injury. They also provide strength and power. Aerobic
exercise improves endurance.

'05 ▼

Football players need to be able to contract their
muscles very rapidly. They need fast, explosive movements
that are fired by their fast-twitch muscle fibers.

Team trainers help develop special exercise programs for their players. An offensive lineman might want to bulk up his upper arms and shoulders. More upper body strength will help him better protect the quarterback. Wide receivers need to be able to generate explosive bursts of speed. A wide receiver might add running sprints and **PLYOMETRICS** to his exercise program.

So how do players get the huge amounts of energy they need to play an intense game? Players once ate protein-rich foods like steak for fuel before a game. Team nutritionists now recommend something heavy in carbohydrates, like pasta. This kind of food is quickly processed into glucose, the body's purest form of fuel.

PLYOMETRICS — exercises that involve rapidly stretching and flexing muscles to produce fast, powerful movements

MAN DOWN

A popular saying goes, "The bigger they are, the harder they fall." The more mass a person has, the greater momentum he builds. When that momentum is suddenly stopped, a person can be injured by the force. As the size of football players has increased, so has the number of injuries.

Explosive running movements cause hamstring tears and pulls. Sudden twisting movements can sprain ankles. Quarterbacks get injuries in their shoulders and elbows from repeatedly throwing the football.

Knee injuries can end a player's career. The anterior cruciate ligament (ACL) is a ligament of the knee. It plays an important role in stabilizing the knee and helps a person change direction quickly. ACLs can be torn when a twisting force is applied to the knee while the foot is planted on the ground. Football players are at risk for torn ACLs because of the **LATERAL** movements they make.

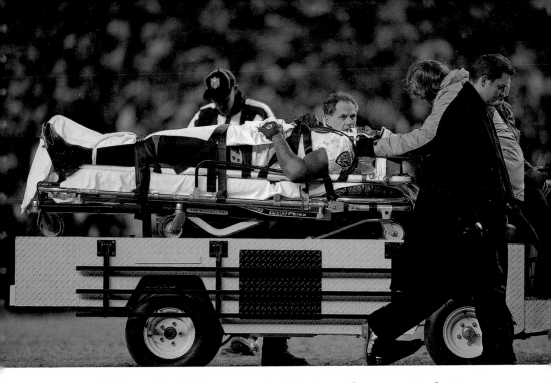

Luckily, medical advances are helping hurt players receive better care than before. Doctors can now repair torn ACLs and damaged shoulder joints without making huge cuts. They use a tiny telescope called an arthroscope to look inside the joint. Arthroscopic surgery doesn't take as long as conventional surgery. Patients also recover more quickly because the surgery doesn't require large cuts.

Football players are being asked to donate their brains to science to research the effect of head impacts.

HEADS UP

Even though players wear helmets, head injuries remain a serious problem for football players. Concussions occur when a hard blow to the head causes the brain to slam against the skull. A severe concussion may cause bleeding inside the brain. When a player suffers a concussion, he becomes more sensitive to future blows to the head. More injuries could eventually cause brain damage.

CHAPTER 6

▷ STADIUMS

Football players play in various conditions. From the turf to the weather to the fans, no two games are alike.

At one time, football was only played on real grass outdoors. But when domed stadiums became popular, things changed. Growing a real grass field under domed conditions is difficult and expensive. People soon started experimenting with different kinds of artificial turf. Astroturf was invented in the 1960s. It got its name after its use at the Houston Astrodome. Soon it was being used in both indoor and outdoor stadiums.

One of the advantages of artificial grass like Astroturf was a consistently level playing field. Fake grass didn't have the dips and holes that real grass had. Those dips could lead to players tripping and getting injured. Artificial turf also lasted longer and didn't need watering and mowing.

But players didn't like the fake stuff. The artificial surfaces were denser. With less give to the field, players developed "turf toe." This injury is similar to jamming your finger, but it happens to your big toe. Astroturf was also rougher than real grass. Players received some bad scrapes from skidding across the ground. Another drawback was the heat of fake turf. The materials in artificial turf absorb light more easily than real grass, which causes fake turf to heat up. On a hot, sunny day, the temperature of fake turf could reach 160 degrees Fahrenheit (71 degrees Celsius).

Newer artificial turfs have eliminated some of the problems found in older kinds of fake turf. But some players still prefer the real stuff to fake grass.

WEATHER WOES

Only nine of the 31 NFL stadiums are domed. That means games are played in all sorts of weather. Players must deal with brutally cold and horribly hot conditions, as well as snow and rain.

▶ INTENSE COLD

Cold temperatures cause muscles to tense up. Tense muscles lessen a player's range of motion and make injuries more likely. During cold games, heaters on the sidelines help players stay loose. Players also wear more layers of clothing to keep warm.

The coldest game in NFL history was nicknamed the "Ice Bowl of 1967." The Green Bay Packers hosted the Dallas Cowboys in Green Bay, Wisconsin. Temperatures dropped to -13 degrees Fahrenheit (-25 degrees Celsius).

► FEELING HOT

Artificial turf isn't the only thing that gets hot in the sun. Hot weather can cause heat cramps, heat exhaustion, and heat stroke. Heat makes muscles that are already tired feel even more exhausted. Combine that with **DEHYDRATION** from sweating, and players can have serious problems. Dizziness, nausea, and feeling faint are all signs of heat-related problems. Players with these symptoms should take a break to cool down and drink up.

► ALTITUDE ADJUSTMENTS

Even how far above sea level a game is played can make a difference. The higher up you go, the more air particles spread apart. Denver's Mile-High Stadium has thinner air than air at sea level. A ball can be kicked slightly farther there.

DEHYDRATION — the condition that occurs when the body does not have enough water

THE CROWD ROARS

Can noisy crowds in a stadium affect the outcome of a football game? Fans believe that loudly cheering for their home team gives their players an advantage. Research supports the idea that crowds can affect athletic performance. But it may not be the effect the fans are hoping for.

HOME FIELD ADVANTAGE

There does appear to be a home field advantage, but it probably doesn't have anything to do with the crowd. Sports psychologists think that playing on home territory is what helps a team perform better. Players on the visiting team may be unfamiliar with the stadium's playing field. They may also be tired from traveling.

Decibels (dB) are used to measure sound intensity. Ten dB is the sound of normal breathing. Forty dB is a buzzing mosquito. Seventy dB is the sound of a vacuum cleaner in action. Most Super Bowl crowds range from 95 to 110 dB.

Cheering fans may actually be doing their team more harm than good. The roar can make it hard for players to hear instructions and can lead to false starts and other miscommunication. Some football crowds can get as loud as 120 dB. This level can actually damage a person's hearing.

Decibel Levels of Certain Sounds

dB	Sound
10	normal breathing
20	rustling leaves
30	whisper
40	buzzing mosquito
50	quiet office
60	normal conversation
70	vacuum cleaner
80	busy traffic
90	Niagara Falls
100	lawn mower
110	heavy construction noise
120	rock concert
130	machine gun
150	jet taking off

But who can blame fans for cheering when they're watching such an exciting, action-packed sport? Knowing the science behind it makes the players' physical feats even more fascinating.

GLOSSARY

acceleration (ak-sel-uh-RAY-shuhn) — the change in speed of a moving body

aerodynamic (ayr-oh-dy-NA-mik) — designed to reduce air resistance

center of gravity (SEN-tur UHV GRAV-uh-tee) — the point on an object at which it can balance

center of mass (SEN-tur UHV MASS) — the point in a body at which most of the mass is concentrated

dehydration (dee-hy-DRAY-shuhn) — the condition that occurs when the body does not have enough water

density (DEN-si-tee) — how heavy an object is for its size; to measure density, divide an object's mass by its volume.

equator (i-KWAY-tuhr) — an imaginary line around the middle of a rounded object

gyroscope (JYE-ruh-skope) — an object that spins inside a frame and causes the frame to balance in any position

hang time (HANG TIME) — how long the ball hangs in the air once it is kicked

intercept (in-tur-SEPT) — when a defensive player catches an offensive pass

lateral (LAT-ur-uhl) — side-to-side

mass (MASS) — the amount of material in an object

plyometrics (ply-uh-MEH-triks) — rapidly stretching and flexing muscles to produce fast, powerful movements

range (RAYNJ) — the distance an object can or does travel

velocity (vuh-LOSS-uh-tee) — a measurement of both the speed and direction an object is moving

READ MORE

Coffland, Jack and David A. Coffland. *Football Math: Touchdown Activities and Projects for Grades 4–8.* Tucson, Ariz.: Good Year Books, 2005.

De Winter, James. *Secrets of Sport: The Technology that Makes Champions.* Extreme! Mankato, Minn.: Capstone Press, 2009.

Levine, Shar, and Leslie Johnstone. *Sports Science.* New York: Sterling Pub., 2006.

Solway, Andrew. *Sports Science.* Why Science Matters. Chicago: Heinemann, 2009.

INTERNET SITES

FactHound offers a safe, fun way to find Internet sites related to this book. All of the sites on Facthound have been researched by our staff.

Here's all you do:

Visit *www.facthound.com*

FactHound will fetch the best sites for you!

INDEX